Original title:
The Language of Leaves

Copyright © 2025 Creative Arts Management OÜ
All rights reserved.

Author: Evelyn Hartman
ISBN HARDBACK: 978-1-80581-711-6
ISBN PAPERBACK: 978-1-80581-238-8
ISBN EBOOK: 978-1-80581-711-6

Whispers of the Woodland

In a forest where trees plot,
Squirrels gossip about the hot spot.
Branches chuckle, leaves play pranks,
All while the mushrooms give thanks.

Breezes carry secrets, oh so light,
Roots reminisce of their last fright.
The acorns roll with a giggle or two,
As the owls wink, 'Oh, who knew?'

Fragments of Green Conversations

Grass blades dance in the sun's glow,
Bumping into rocks, putting on a show.
"Leaf it to me!" says one with a grin,
While vines tease the saplings, 'Let's spin!'

The ferns shuffle, oh what a sight,
Whispering tales deep into the night.
"Did you hear the story of the beetle's bling?"
"Next time, we'll wear crowns, let's be the king!"

Secrets Written in Canopy Lines

High above, the branches sway,
Chatting about the humans' silly play.
"Did you see that one trip and fumble?"
"Bet he'll blame it on the jungle!"

Leaves flutter, sharing a wink,
As the birds laugh, "We need a drink!"
Moss giggles softly, feeling quite sly,
While shadows twirl, oh me, oh my!

Treetops' Silent Symphony

In the treetops, a melody brews,
Branches strum to the morning blues.
"Look at that squirrel, can't catch his tail!"
"Maybe he thinks he's a ship in sail!"

Whispering leaves begin to hum,
"Here comes the wind, oh what fun!"
The sky blushes, a joyful cheer,
As the woodland band strikes up, oh dear!

Notes from Nature's Notebook

In the breeze, whispers call,
A squirrel's jest, a hearty brawl.
Leaves giggle, twirl, and sway,
As branches dance by the bay.

A crow croaks out a clever pun,
While sunlight bathes us, oh what fun!
Trees gossip, sharing their tales,
While roots weave stories like old trails.

Observations Through the Arbor

A caterpillar in a hat,
Claims he'll fly, imagine that!
Raccoons don masks at night,
Their masked ball, a comical sight.

Breezes hum a catchy tune,
While owls dance under the moon.
Branches creak with laughter's hint,
Nature's jesters, never mint.

Traces of Treetop Thoughts

Acorns drop like little bombs,
Each thud, sweet nature's charms.
A woodpecker's knocking spree,
Making music, oh so free.

Pine needles wear a sappy grin,
Tickled by the playful wind.
In every rustle, a chuckle hides,
Nature's humor, the world abides.

Imprints on the Ground

Footprints left by a woeful hare,
Dancing round without a care.
Mushrooms pop, they're quite the show,
Winking at all who stroll below.

Grassy carpets host leaf debates,
While crickets chirp, their own updates.
Nature's stage, a wacky site,
Where every critter's life's delight.

Leafy Letters

In a forest where secrets are spun,
Leaves whisper tales, oh, what fun!
They giggle and flutter, they dance in the sun,
Sharing riddles of how the day's begun.

A maple writes softly in shades of red,
While the oak tells a joke, sitting up in his bed.
A birch rolls her eyes at the drama ahead,
Caught in the breeze, the laughter widespread.

Nature's Epistles

Overhead the branches scribble a note,
To squirrels who scamper and find a good coat.
A fern hands a message, quite fluffy and float,
"Don't forget to water the roots, or we'll gloat!"

A dandelion dreams in the swirl of the air,
While wind sends replies, dancing wild without care.
Each petal's a word, spun without a snare,
The forest's a postman, delivering flair.

Gestures of Growth

The seedlings stretch out with a wave and a cheer,
Reaching for sunlight, they've no hint of fear.
The flowers are gossiping, all too sincere,
"Did you hear what the thistle said? Oh dear!"

Roots high-five underground, tease the grass so green,
"Look at us stretching, we're real growing machines!"
A cactus grins broadly, with no need for a screen,
As nature's own jesters play out on the scene.

The Tale of Wind and Wood

Once a breeze met a branch in a quirky affair,
Whirling and twirling, dancing without a care.
"Let's write a story," the wind did declare,
"Of all the tall tales that branches could share!"

The wood laughed and nodded, they plotted and schemed,

Under the moonlight, so silly, it seemed.
"With leaves as our ink, we can dream and redeem,
And turn all the chuckles to a wondrous theme!"

Illuminated by Nature's Palette

Colorful whispers dance on the breeze,
Leaves giggle softly in playful tease.
A red one steps out, adorned with flair,
While green ones hide behind, feeling bare.

Crisp maple chatter, crisp and bright,
Competing for laughs, they take to flight.
A yellow leaf spins, a pirouette soon,
While the brown one grumbles, "Just give me a tune!"

Poems of the Seasons

In spring, the buds are like poets in bloom,
Each one reciting love with a plume.
Summer's lush laughter, bold and loud,
Brings out the silly from nature's crowd.

Autumn sings songs of rustling cheer,
Whispers of crunch underfoot, oh dear!
Winter's hush brings a giggle or two,
As snowflakes tickle noses, just for you.

Whims of Whisking Wind

Oh, the breeze plays tricks with a teasing whiff,
Twirling leaves 'round, a light-hearted skiff.
"Catch me if you can!" the oak tree shouts,
While gusts of laughter echo, no doubts.

Swirling through branches, a game of tag,
The wind steals hats, oh what a rag!
In its playful grasp, each leaf takes flight,
Whisking away, they vanish from sight.

Conversations in the Canopy

Under the branches, where chatter takes place,
Leaves share their secrets with humor and grace.
A sassy little sprout pipes up with glee,
"Did you hear the one about the old oak tree?"

The wise walnut chuckles, "Oh I've got a tale,
About a rosebush who wanted to sail!"
Laughter erupts as the stories unfold,
In the leafy gathering, hilarity bold.

Syllables in the Shimmer

In the morning light they dance,
Telling secrets with a prance.
A leaf that wiggles, two that sway,
Whispering gossip, come what may.

They chuckle softly as they tease,
Tickling branches with the breeze.
"Look at him, that old oak tree!"
"His leaves are drooping, oh, so free!"

Laughter ripples through the green,
A playful sight, a lovely scene.
One leaf jokes, "I've lost my edge!"
Another shouts, "Just join the hedge!"

In autumn's glow, they share a jest,
"Who's the funniest? We're the best!"
Crisp laughter as they flutter down,
Nature's jesters in this crown.

Echoes Beneath the Bark

In whispers deep, the stories dwell,
Beneath the bark, where secrets swell.
The squirrels eavesdrop, giggle loud,
As trees share tales that make them proud.

"Remember when that branch was new?"
"Ha! A twig, that's nothing, boo!"
Leaves chime in with a rustling cheer,
"Your puns are fine but gives me fear!"

A squirrel pipes, "I'm quite the poet!"
The trees reply, "Oh, please don't show it!"
Acorns laugh, rolling around,
As the whole forest joins in sound.

Beneath the bark, let humor flow,
Wise old trees put on a show.
"Let's drop some leaves and make a scene!"
Nature's jesters, bright and green.

Pages of Rustling Stories

Flipping pages in the breeze,
Whispered tales among the trees.
"Did you hear about the spindly vine?"
"It couldn't climb, but always signed!"

A leaf adorned in polka dots,
Said, "I'm a star, like it or not!"
Their laughter swirls—what fun to share,
Nature's laughter fills the air.

The petals gossip, stick a tongue,
"Let's have a party, come, ye young!"
They wiggle and giggle in the sun,
Each rustling whisper a pun begun.

Around they spin, in joy they sway,
Every leaf has something to say.
In nature's book, let humor reign,
Rustling tales, like sweet champagne.

The Soliloquy of Foliage

Oh, stands the maple, proud and bright,
Quoting lines from day to night.
"Why do birds always get to sing?"
"I'd rather dance, that's my fling!"

"Is it autumn yet? I'm feeling bold!"
"Not yet, my friend, let summer hold!"
A witty breeze chimes in to say,
"Patience now, it's still today!"

A leaf with style, quite dapper, too,
Spins a tale that's fancy and new.
With every rustle, laughter flows,
Chasing dreams where humor grows.

In nature's realm, let joy recur,
Every leaf a quirky blur.
A leafy soliloquy unfolds,
In chuckles, nature's heart enfolds.

The Flight of Flora

In a breeze, the petals fly,
Dancing high, oh me, oh my!
Squirrels stop, then start to laugh,
At flowers taking a wacky path.

Butterflies with silly grins,
Flutter 'round, chasing their kin.
A daisy lands on a wild hare,
'This isn't home!' it seems to declare.

Dandelions whisper, 'We can't stop!'
While robins gather all the crop.
Leaves spin like they've got no care,
'Catch me if you can!' they dare.

Amidst the giggles, the sun shines bright,
In this joyful, leafy flight.
Watch as nature spills its glee,
In the air, so wild and free!

Silhouettes Against the Sky

At dusk, the trees play peek-a-boo,
Shadows twist, a comical view.
Branches wiggle, greet the night,
As squirrels clap in sheer delight.

A raccoon waves, his mask in place,
While bushes bow with dainty grace.
The moon a spectator in the fun,
As owls gossip, 'Who's number one?'

Breezes stretch, tickle the boughs,
As crickets sing their nightly vows.
They chirp and laugh, compete for cheer,
'This is our stage! Let's take a beer!'

With every rustle, the trees declare,
'Life's a comedy, so don't you dare
Miss this show in the cool twilight,
Where silhouettes dance 'til morning light!'

The Dance of the Forest

In the forest, leaves perform,
A jig that breaks the standard norm.
Twisting left and leaping right,
They host a party all night!

Mossy roots tap on the ground,
Each stomp a joy, a vibrant sound.
A bushy tail swings to and fro,
As critters join the leafy show.

The branches wave a happy dance,
Inviting all for a merry prance.
Toadstools form a conga line,
'Fungi fun, it's our time to shine!'

As dawn approaches, they don't quite fade,
Still spinning in a leafy parade.
In this forest, laughter reigns,
Where the joy of nature entertains!

Evergreen Eulogies

The pines chant in tones so light,
They rib each other, 'What a sight!'
With needles sharp, they poke and tease,
'Ever green, but allergies, please!'

Fir trees boast of their height and girth,
While spruces sing of their noble worth.
'We're the best at holding snow!'
– A humorous claim, they'd surely show.

Barking trees share jokes from years deep,
As leaves rustle, they can hardly keep.
A comic sketch of winter's jest,
'Let's compete to see who's dressed the best!'

Through laughter and a gentle sway,
In this grove, they cherish the play.
With evergreen smiles, they never grieve,
For every moment's a chance to believe!

The Script of Swaying Branches

In branches swaying, secrets play,
With whispers soft, they dance all day.
A leaf stops, then it shakes its head,
"You thought I'd fall? Not yet!" it said.

A squirrel's giggle, a rustle near,
"I'll wear you all like a fashion sneer!"
One leaf replies, in a cheeky tone,
"But in a breeze, I'm not alone!"

They twirl and spin, a leafy show,
"Hold on tight! Here comes the blow!"
As gusts of wind give them a lift,
"Catch us if you can! Here's our gift!"

So watch these leaves with a teasing grin,
For every sway is a game to win.
In laughter green, their voices swell,
A merry tale that leaves us well.

Ballads of Bloom and Fade

In spring we sing of colors bright,
A bloom that dances, pure delight.
Petals whisper, "Winter's done!"
"Let's party hard, it'll be so fun!"

But summer comes with scorching beams,
"Hey folks, remember our dreams?"
Flowers giggle, "We're still alive!"
"Well, shine on high, let's all survive!"

Autumn's call, a rustling cheer,
"Let's pile the leaves, the best of the year!"
With colors bold, they take a dive,
"In crunchy chaos, we feel alive!"

Then winter swoops, and all goes grey,
Yet still they joke, come join our play!
"We fade, but wait! We'll be back soon!"
In every season, a funny tune!

The Dialogue of Seasons

In spring, the flowers giggle,
As the sun tries to tickle.
The trees nod with delight,
While squirrels dance in the light.

Summer shouts, 'Let's sunbathe!'
While birds chirp, 'Here's a wave!'
A bee buzzes with glee,
'Join the party, just be free!'

Fall arrives in a swirl,
With leaves in a cheeky twirl.
The pumpkins grin so wide,
As acorns giggle and hide.

Winter's frosty laugh rings,
While snowflakes wear fuzzy rings.
The pines shake off their frost,
And shout, "Who's having a frost?"

Odes to the Orchard

In the orchard, apples cheer,
Telling tales the squirrels hear.
'We shine so bright and red!'
Said one with a shiny head.

Pears giggle on their limbs,
'We're the ones with fancy whims!'
Bouncing on the breezes,
Playing games like little sea-fleas.

Cherries snicker from above,
'Don't steal our fruit, it's tough love!'
While blossoms blush with flair,
'We brighten days beyond compare!'

Plums roll down, playing tag,
With a little, silly wag.
Laughs echo in the shade,
As sweet memories are made.

Murmurs in the Meadow

In the meadow, grasses sway,
Telling secrets day by day.
Butterflies wear silly hats,
While hopping around with chats.

Daisies shout, 'Look at me!'
While bees dance, full of glee.
'Pollinate, let's have fun!'
Said the flower, nearly spun.

Hares hop with a funny face,
Chasing each other in a race.
'Catch me if you can!' they say,
As they bounce and skip away.

Clouds above begin to grin,
As raindrops tease to come in.
But the sun makes a bright scene,
'Let's party here, it's so green!'

Metaphors in Every Vein

In the forest, whispers play,
Woodpeckers tap the day away.
Trees joke about their height,
'Who's the tallest? What a sight!'

Vines giggle like old friends,
Winding up, where laughter bends.
Leaves speak in shades so bold,
Tales of spring and memories told.

Rabbits tease in leafy dress,
Playing hide-and-seek, no less.
While oaks hold their heads up high,
'We keep secrets, oh my my!'

Flowers sprinkle jokes so light,
In colors, they choose to ignite.
Nature sings its cheeky tune,
As the stars peek out at noon.

Verses in Verdant Hues

In the park where grasses grow,
Leaves gossip softly, row by row.
A tree sneezes, leaves take flight,
Wondering if they'll be alright.

Squirrels chatter, full of cheer,
Arguing who's the bravest here.
A leaf flips, showing its back,
Winking at bugs who don't cut slack.

Branches wave in breezy jest,
Who's the finest? They'll all contest.
A maple teases the oak nearby,
'Your shade can't hide a squirrel's sly!'

With each rustle, a pun unfolds,
In whispers of green, fun never grows old.

Conversations in the Canopy

Up high where the rich green sways,
Trees exchange their quirky ways.
'Did you see that bird's wild dance?'
'Yeah, but I didn't get a chance!'

A leaf declares it's got a plan,
To tickle a cheeky forest span.
The branches chuckle, 'What a sight!'
A twig says, 'You're too light tonight!'

They scheme a laugh over winds that spin,
'Let's sway to a tune, let the fun begin!'
Vines twirl like ribbons, sprightly and grand,
While acorns chuckle, 'Isn't life just bland?'

When dusk falls, their laughter stays,
Echos of joy in the leafy maze.

Silent Stanzas of the Forest

In a hush where shadows play,
Leaves chuckle in a cheeky way.
'Did you hear that old tree's joke?'
It's one of those that always poke!

A pine needles in, quite dry,
'My sense of humor is a bit shy.'
But as a breeze blows through the grove,
It whispers nothing but the love!

Old roots snicker beneath the floor,
'How many trees does it take to soar?'
But leaves just shimmy, showing flair,
For laughter spreads through cool pine air!

A gentle sway, a quiet jest,
In this garden, how we are blessed!

Shade's Subtle Sonnets

Underneath the leafy cloak,
Foliage weaves a comedy yoke.
'Leafy, you're looking quite green!'
'Thank you, it's my seasonal sheen!'

A dapple of sunlight joins the fun,
'Who'll tell the best pun by run?'
The lilac whispers, 'I'm in the race!'
While daisies bloom with smirks on their face.

They twist and twirl in playful greets,
Roots joke about their tangled feats.
'Hey tree, do you leaf your worries?'
'Only when the wind stirs frenzies!'

In the shadowed nooks, giggles thrive,
Where every leaf finds a reason to jive!

Whispers of the Canopy

Branches sway with glee,
Telling tales of sunny spree.
Squirrels giggle, acorns fall,
Nature's jesters, one and all.

A leaf turns red, says, "Look at me!"
While others laugh, "You're just a tree!"
The wind bursts out in fits of cheer,
Tickling bark, it's time to steer.

Wise old tree, with trunk so stout,
Chuckles softly, wisps about.
"Why so serious?" it seems to say,
"Just laugh as you dance the day away!"

So join the leaves in playful spin,
Forget your woes, let joy begin.
For in the boughs, both high and low,
Laughter blooms where the breezes blow.

Conversations with Autumn

What's that crunch? A friendly greet,
Pumpkins giggle at my feet.
A yellow leaf shouts, "I'm the star!"
"Please don't fall! You're near too far!"

The acorns sing, a merry tune,
While trees plot mischief 'neath the moon.
"Grab your coats, it's sweater weather!"
"Let's flare up the fun altogether!"

"Who will win the wind's wild race?"
"Bet on the leaf with the greenest face!"
Autumn chuckles, collects lost bets,
As laughter echoes, no regrets.

So raise a toast with cider sweet,
Together here, life is a treat.
The season winks, the sun shines bright,
In this lively chat 'neath autumn's light.

Tales Written in Green

In a garden where whispers grow,
A leaf tells secrets, don't you know?
"It's not about roots or the bark,
But tales of love in the spark!"

The dandelions giggle and sway,
"Gossip's fresh, be on your way!"
With each rustle, they share a plot,
"Did you see the snail? What a lot!"

Butterflies flit, with colors bright,
"Listen close! We sing all night!"
The flowers chime in, a colorful crew,
"Who needs a stage? We've got a view!"

So come dear friend to this green embrace,
Join in the laughter, pick up the pace.
In every leaf, there's joy to glean,
In this funny world, where grass is green.

Secrets Beneath the Bark

Beneath the bark, there's quite a scene,
Where wise old fungi plot and scheme.
They gossip softly, secrets shared,
In this dark world, no one's spared.

"No more rain! Or else we drown!"
One toadstool sighs, while wearing a crown.
"Let's throw a party, light it up!"
As roots entwine and dance in sup.

The worms join in with wiggle-wag,
"Keep it down, we can't lag!"
But laughter bursts! It can't be tamed,
In this secret life, none are blamed.

And as the sun peeks through the trees,
All join in, "We'll do as we please!"
With every giggle and friendly bark,
There's joy found here, in the darkest park.

The Story of Every Leaf

In the breeze, they love to dance,
Whispering secrets, taking a chance.
Some are big, and some are small,
They flutter down, without a recall.

Chasing squirrels, playing hide and seek,
Laughing as raindrops make them squeak.
In circles they twirl, a playful bunch,
Napping together, a leafy lunch.

Each twist and turn, a giggling sound,
Rolling along, they tumble around.
In autumn's glow, they take a bow,
Falling in style, oh wow, look now!

They gossip of storms, share tales of sun,
The tales never stop; oh, there's always fun.
So next time you pass a tree so tall,
Remember, those leaves have seen it all!

Echoes of Ebb and Flow

Raindrops giggle as they land,
Leaves reply with a rustling stand.
Dancing puddles, splishing and splashing,
Nature's laughter, forever dashing.

The river sings with a bubbly tune,
As branches sway like a funky cartoon.
Frogs join in with a ribbit and croak,
Swaying together, they share a joke.

When the sun shines, they bask in glee,
Spinning tales of what they see.
A dragonfly zooms, then stops for tea,
Nature's comedy, so vibrant and free.

As waves crash softly on sandy shores,
Leaves whisper secrets like old folklore.
In every rustle, a chuckle, a smile,
Echoes of joy that go on for a while.

Ties Between Trunks

Two trunks meet in a hug so tight,
Cracking jokes from morning to night.
Vines climb up with a tickle and tease,
Sharing laughter with the buzzing bees.

Roots tangle deep, like old friends' grasp,
Holding on tight, they whisper and clasp.
Together they sway, what a sight to see,
Spreading cheer like a leafy jubilee.

Squirrels scamper, lovebirds sing,
Nature's party, oh what joy they bring!
Each knot and twist, a tale they weave,
It's not just trees; they're family, believe!

Beneath the moon, whispers take flight,
Gather 'round trunks, it's storytelling night.
With giggles and jests, they celebrate,
In the roots of friendship, they resonate.

Nature's Narrative

A leaf fell down with a silly swoosh,
Flapping and flailing, it gave a whoosh!
It whispered tales of branches high,
With each flutter, it tried to fly.

In the forest, every leaf has flair,
From dancing around to the playful air.
They twiddle their stems and share a grin,
As critters laugh, and the stories begin.

Breezes tease in a playful race,
Leaves join in with a hilarious chase.
Tiptoeing softly down the bark,
Knocking on wood, leaving a mark.

And when autumn paints the scene,
Leaves wear colors fit for a queen.
They crack witty puns on the way down,
In nature's joke fest, they wear a crown!

The Chorus of Changing Tides

The ocean sings a silly tune,
Waves dance like cats beneath the moon.
Seagulls squawking jokes from the sky,
While sand crabs giggle as they scurry by.

Shells wear hats from yesterday's feast,
Each find a treasure, a quirky beast.
Tide pools are mirrors, reflecting glee,
As fishy friends chat in watery spree.

Jellyfish giggle, floating in grace,
While starfish tease, 'Look at my face!'
Barnacles whisper, 'We're fashionable too!'
All join together in this silly brew.

So come hear the laughter, don't be shy,
Where the waves tell tales and sea creatures fly.
Join the chorus where tides collide,
In this happy ocean, let joy be your guide.

A Tapestry of Tangled Thoughts

In the forest where squirrels plot,
Their acorn stash is a laughing lot.
Trees gossip softly about the breeze,
Whispering secrets beneath twisted leaves.

Rabbits wear glasses, reading a map,
Finding their way or taking a nap?
While hedgehogs spin tales of daring deeds,
In a world where imagination leads.

The mushrooms nod in their polka dot suits,
As flowers dance in their colorful boots.
A butterfly flutters, tipsy with glee,
Saying, 'Hey bugs, just follow me!'

Laughter erupts from the thickets nearby,
As nature's creatures let out a cry.
A tapestry woven from joy and delight,
All tangled up in the soft moonlight.

Whispers in Fall's Embrace

Leaves tumble down with a sassy flair,
Like dancers twirling, light as air.
Crunchy carpets make for a show,
As kids leap in piles, laughing down low.

The trees play peek-a-boo with delight,
As pumpkins smile, all round and bright.
Squirrels chatter about nuts galore,
While frogs croak jokes at the forest floor.

A breeze teases whispers through branches high,
Tickling cheeky crows up in the sky.
Nature's punchlines echo and sway,
In this funny autumn ballet.

So grab your scarf and join the fun,
With leaves in the air, life's never done.
In fall's embrace, laughter befalls,
Every moment's a giggle beneath the stalls.

Nature's Unspoken Rhapsody

In meadows lush where daisies play,
A goat hums low, 'What's the word of the day?'
Bumblebees buzz with tales to tell,
While ants form parades—it's quite the swell!

Clouds gather for a fluffy debate,
Casting shadows and maybe some fate.
Rabbits hop in rhythm, all out of time,
While frogs in the pond splash with a rhyme.

Ferns fan away gossip from the ground,
While ladybugs waltz without making a sound.
Crickets compose their nightly song,
In a world where nature just rolls along.

So listen closely, if you dare,
To the rhapsody played in the open air.
A symphony played by forgotten hosts,
In the wild where laughter matters the most.

Ballads of the Wilderness

In the woods where squirrels dance,
Leaves gossip in a breezy trance.
Trees crack jokes, oh what a sight,
Whispering secrets, day and night.

Beneath a bough, a rabbit sighs,
Hoping for lunch, or at least some fries.
The roots laugh low, in earthy cheer,
While birds trade puns, and lend an ear.

A raccoon donning a tiny hat,
Catches a glimpse of a chubby cat.
Branches rustle, teasing the breeze,
What a hoot, these woodland committees!

As twilight falls, the fireflies flick,
Playing pranks with their tiny tricks.
In the wild, where all is wacky,
Nature's humor is truly snappy.

The Gift of Green

A sprout pops up with a cheeky grin,
Saying, "Watch me now, I'll grow like sin!"
With every gust, it wiggles free,
Join my party, come laugh with me!

Vines twist and twirl in a leafy dance,
Claiming the world with a daring stance.
They tickle the noses of passing deer,
While branches chuckle, 'Oh dear, oh dear!'

In a garden, a gnome starts to sway,
With sunflowers sharing their bright ballet.
"Watch this!" he shouts, as he pirouettes,
Leaves join in, and forget their debts.

Even cacti join the jovial song,
Bouncing around, oh, where they belong!
Nature's joyful, a playful scheme,
Each green giggle, a whimsical dream.

Chants of the Evergreen

Pine trees whisper in hushed delight,
Crafting jokes to last through the night.
"Why did the leaf fall?" asks one sage,
"To get to the root of the leafy stage!"

Beneath the boughs, a bear stops by,
Hilarious tales make the branches sigh.
While owls wink with their wise old eyes,
Spreading laughter beneath starlit skies.

Needles tickle, all in good jest,
Nature's humor shines at its best.
The wind howls softly, and joins the fun,
In a playful chorus, everyone's won!

Evergreens chuckle, holding their ground,
With every chuckle, joy abounds.
In their embrace, the world finds peace,
While silly stories never cease.

Visions of Verdant Lore

In a glade where fungi rhyme,
To the rhythm of nature's prime.
Mushrooms dance with a giddy spin,
Claiming the daisies, all to win!

A beetle challenges a flying bug,
To a race around an old tree rug.
With each twist and turn, they start to tease,
Beneath the shade of fluttering leaves.

Frogs croak loudly, their own charade,
Upstaging crickets in leafy parade.
While fireflies light, a comedic show,
Nature's wit is all aglow.

In this green realm, laughter is law,
From creeping vines, to creatures in awe.
With every giggle, the forest thrives,
Spreading joy, where humor derives.

Leaves Speak in Colors

In summer shades of green, they play,
Whispering secrets in a bright ballet.
They giggle in the breeze, a rustling cheer,
Dancing with joy for all trees near.

When autumn shows up, they turn to gold,
Telling jokes of warmth, bold and old.
Scarlet clashes with orange, what a sight!
"Who wore it best?" they ask in delight.

Winter arrives, they take a break,
Crisp and crunchy, for fun's sake.
They laugh at snowflakes, such silly friends,
Joking about how the fun never ends.

Nature's Written Serenade

In the breeze, they ruffle tunes,
Crafting ballads under the moons.
Each flutter brings a funny rhyme,
Nature's jesters, keeping time.

They sing of squirrels and their nuts,
Laugh at grounding birds with struts.
"Look at me," a leaf might brag,
"I'm the punchline; better than a rag!"

As raindrops fall, they splash and play,
Sliding down in a leaf parade.
"Watch us surf!" they giggle and float,
On a river of laughter, they happily gloat.

The Poetics of Petiole

Petiole stands up tall with pride,
Swinging leaves, a leafy guide.
"Who needs roots when you can sway?"
They shake their stems, it's a leafy ballet.

Quirky shapes with wit aplenty,
Some leaves are round, others just dandy.
"Look at my haircut," they jest,
Each one's a fashionista at its best!

When wind blows in, they hold a fest,
LOLs and ROFLs, it's their quest.
"Catch me if you can, clever gnome!"
And off they dance, far from their home.

Rustling Rhythms of Earth

Rustling lightly, they have their beat,
Nature's band on every street.
With each breeze, they chime along,
Creating that joyful leaf song.

They crackle like chips underfoot,
Making mischief, oh, what a hoot!
"Leave it to us," they jingle and jive,
In a world where they truly thrive.

With rhythms so silly, they cause a stir,
Tickling bushes, who start to purr.
Leaves and laughter, a perfect blend,
Spreading cheer, never to end!

Tints and Tones of Nature's Verse

Crimson whispers float like jokes,
The grass giggles and croaks.
Leaves chirp tales with fluttering glee,
A dance of hues, come laugh with me.

In the sun, gold puns abound,
On branches, laughter can be found.
Nature's palette, wild and free,
Shades of mirth from A to Z.

Foliage tickles with vibrant flair,
Sassy squirrels strike a pose in the air.
A leafy banquet, all dressed in green,
With nature's humor, it's quite the scene.

Here in this green comedy so divine,
Even the moss has a punchline.
So join the show, it's quite a spree,
In every leaf, a joke, you see!

Sonnet of the Seasons

Spring throws a party, blooms in a fray,
With flowers dressed like they've come out to play.
Summer's heat makes sunflowers tilt,
They bask in rays, as if by quilt.

Autumn chuckles, dropping leaves with style,
Like confetti, it's a vibrant free-for-all mile.
Winter sneezes, hoarfrost laughs and clings,
While birds share gossip on their frosty wings.

Each season shares its quirky flair,
With nature's banter hanging in the air.
Round the clock, the jokes take root,
In every whisper of leaf or shoot.

So turn the page in this merry tale,
Nature's antics will always prevail.
From budding scripts to frosty puns,
The seasons dance, and laughter runs.

The Dialect of Timid Breezes

Breezes tiptoe, shy yet spry,
Whispering secrets as they pass by.
Leaves giggle softly, rustling their dress,
In a gentle breeze, they find happiness.

Timid winds play hide and seek,
Giggling through branches, clever and cheeky.
The trees sway, a dance of delight,
With a fluttering chuckle, the world feels light.

A tickle from the gusty air,
Leaves chuckle softly without a care.
In the stillness, a giggle starts,
In the heart of leaves, are joyful parts.

So catch a breeze in jest and fun,
Nature's humor has just begun.
Join the frolic, let laughter flow,
With whispers of leaves, come feel the glow!

Chronicles in Chlorophyll

In green-hued scripts, the stories unfold,
Tales of sunshine and raindrops bold.
Leaves gather 'round, sharing jest,
Each frond a character, nature's best.

A leaf wrote a memoir, funny and bright,
Of wind-blown blunders and blight of the light.
Roots chuckle below, plumbing the dirt,
While blossoms gossip, with petals to flirt.

The whispers of foliage weave a tale,
Of cheeky squirrels and a bright-eyed snail.
Nestled in shade, laughter does bloom,
As nature spins yarns in leafy rooms.

So read the scrolls of chlorophyll bright,
Join in the fun; it's a glorious sight.
Each leaf a storyteller, so full of glee,
In this green realm, come stay, be free!

Stories of Sunlight and Shadow

In the garden, leaves debate,
Who's the best at looking great.
One claims it's all about the style,
While another just says, "Wait a while!"

Dancing gently with the breeze,
They chuckle softly, aiming to please.
A sunbeam says, "I'll steal the show!"
A shadow replies, "Just watch me glow!"

Green gossip travels far and wide,
Every whisper filled with pride.
Branches lean in, all ears on deck,
As sunlight throws jokes like a speck.

With each rustling laugh they share,
The backyard turns a lively fair.
A secret club of leafy cheer,
Where the punchline is always near.

Phrases in Petals

The petals shout in vibrant hues,
"Choose me! I'm the one to amuse!"
They flirt with bees, a lovely game,
While laughing loudly – who's to blame?

With a twist and a twirl so bright,
They boast of tales in day and night.
"I'm the prettiest!" one flower claims,
While others just giggle at their names.

Poetry in every bloom,
Cheeky whispers, none of them gloom.
The scents they share are sweet and light,
As butterflies join in their flight.

A vibrant discussion, petals agree,
Life's too short to simply be.
So with smiles, they join the sun,
In a rhyme where all has fun.

Sonnet of Swaying Branches

Branches swaying with a laugh,
Each one boasts, "I'm the biggest staff!"
They jabber on in a leafy haze,
Taking turns to share their praise.

The oak says, "Look at my strong frame!"
While the willow chimes in with a name.
"I dance like no one else, it's true!"
"But I've got shade, now what about you?"

The pines are straight, but inward jest,
"It's the height that weaves the best quest!"
And with every sway, they point and tease,
An uproar of laughter amidst the leaves.

Fun times in the sway and shake,
Creating laughter, no mistake!
In the forest's heart, let's unite,
As branches blend in pure delight.

Verses in the Veins

In veins of green, a story flows,
Each leaf tells tales that nobody knows.
With whispers of wind and cheeky grins,
The fun begins where the laughter spins.

Little critters stop to hear,
Every line wrapped in cheer.
"Did you hear?" a leaf does say,
"I saw a squirrel run away!"

Veins hold secrets, soft and sly,
Like hidden jokes, they float and fly.
Each fluttering blush a comic act,
While lullabies keep them intact.

In knotted whispers, roots agree,
Let's spin our tales, come dance with me!
For life is a jest, just look outside,
The verses speak; let humor abide!

Dialogues with the Breeze

A leaf in my hair, it dances with glee,
Whispering secrets, just between you and me.
"Catch me if you can!" it teases with flair,
As I swat at the air, I can't find it there.

The wind tells a joke, and the branches all laugh,
A twig slipped on a rock, took a tumble, a gaffe.
"Don't branch out too far!" the oak starts to shout,
As I chuckle and grin, while the leaves spin about.

A squirrel joins in, with a leaf as his hat,
He winks at a butterfly, then flattens flat.
They giggle and chatter, a whimsical band,
Oh, the comic capers, that nature has planned!

So next time you stroll through a breezy old grove,
Listen close to the tales that the foliage wove.
For behind every flutter, and rustle you hear,
Laughter is nestled in each leafy sphere.

Messages from the Treetops

In the heights of the trees, where the chatter's a buzz,
A pinecone declares, "I'm the one with the fuzz!"
The aspen joins in, with a rattle and shake,
"Your spikiness bothers me, for goodness' sake!"

Maple blows kisses from her crimson crown,
"Hey there, Mr. Oak, don't you dare wear that frown!"
The sycamore quips, "You look rather stout,
Have you heard that the rain makes your bark peel out?"

A gust sends the chatter to the ground with a swirl,
And down drifts a note from a leaf-shaped girl.
It reads, "When you're rusty, just dance in the sun!
For each droplet that falls is a reason for fun!"

So next time you gaze at the high leafy quirk,
Remember their banter, the joy from their work.
For amidst photosynthesis, laughter has bloomed,
In a world of green whispers, the joy is presumed.

Verses in the Rustling

A rustle and ruffle, the leaves start to sigh,
"I thought I saw a rabbit, oh my, oh my!"
They gossip and flutter, in their green little way,
"Gnomes love to nap 'neath our shade every day!"

A critter hops by, and the leaves make a scene,
"Is that a fancy squirrel or a bear in between?"
"It's just a raccoon, with a cookie to munch,
Do be polite, and don't scare off his lunch!"

They chatter of seasons, of sunshine and snow,
"What happened to summer? Did you see it go?"
Whispers of autumn, with colors so bright,
"We're just getting started, oh what a delight!"

So stroll with a smile through each whisper and song,
For the rustling of leaves will keep you all day long.
In the joys of each season, nature's cozy embrace,
The playful leaf language, a funny little space.

Lyrics in Lush

In the thicket of green, where all giggles commence,
The leaves form a choir, in melodic suspense.
With each wind that floats by, they sway sharp and sweet,

"I'm the star of the show!" cries the flower's small feat.

A dandelion whispers, "I've stories to share!"
"Of fluffs in the wind and the sun's golden glare.
Just watch as I tumble, I sing with the breeze,
Join in on the fun! Let's play games with the trees!"

The lilacs then chime, with their own fragrant rhymes,
"Forget all your worries, just laugh at the times!"
Their petals are dancing, a waltz in the air,
While giggles erupt, with no need for a care.

So venture out yonder, where the lush greenery grows,
Join in their fun, let your light-heartedness flow.
For in each leafy lyric, a chuckle's found true,
In nature's own playground, there's laughter for you.

Timeless Texts of the Trees

In whispers soft the branches sway,
The gossip travels day by day.
"Did you see that squirrel dance?"
"Oh yes! He's got no sense of chance!"

With every leaf a tale unfolds,
Of ancient stories yet untold.
"Come try the nut that's big and round!"
"It's not a nut, it's lost and found!"

When wind sings sweet, the trunks all sway,
They chuckle loud at kids at play.
"Look at that human, dressed so fine!"
"Is that a hat or shade divine?"

Each rustling leaf, a jester's grin,
In nature's court, we all can win.
"Why did the branch refuse to fly?"
"Too busy laughing at the sky!"

The Leaf's Lament

Oh woe is me, I'm stuck on ground,
Fell from my tree without a sound.
"Can you believe it? What a fall!"
"Don't fret my friend, it's not so tall!"

I watch the dance of breezy bliss,
"Get up! Get up! Don't end like this!"
"Just look at them, the ones that float,
They wave goodbye, but never gloat."

With every step, I swear I see,
A thousand friends have fallen free.
"Gather 'round, it's not the end!"
"We'll start a club, it's leaf to bend!"

So here we are, a leafy crew,
With laughter loud, we shade the blue.
"Who's next to fall? A game we'll play!"
"Let's tumble down, it's tree-lovey day!"

Odes to the Orchard

In orchards bright, where critters roam,
There's always room for fun at home.
"Pick me a fruit, it's ripe and round!"
"Or just pretend that you are a clown!"

The apples giggle, pears just sway,
As giggling kids munch night and day.
"Is that a snack? Oh, don't be shy!"
"It's fruit-o-licious, come and try!"

The branches lower, sharing their glee,
"Let's have a laugh, just you and me."
"What's that you say? A joke from you?"
"Yes, why'd the orange turn blue?"

In every bite, a chuckle hides,
With every crunch, joyous abides.
"Oh orchard lovely, full of cheer!"
"Let's plant a joke for all to hear!"

Remnants of Rustic Rhyme

In meadows wide, where daisies prance,
The grass will sway in a funny dance.
"Look at that bee, so chubby and neat!"
"Buzzing along, can't find his seat!"

Beneath the ferns critters exchange,
Their quirky tales, all kinds of strange.
"Ever seen a snail sing a tune?"
"No, but I bet it plays at noon!"

The owls at night, they gossip away,
On silly things that happened in the day.
"Why did the bat refuse to fly?"
"Too busy laughing at the moon high!"

So here's to nature's funny plight,
In every leaf lies pure delight.
"Let's gather round, the show's about!"
"Join us, friend, we'll laugh it out!"

Syllables in the Shade

In the grove where laughter's pure,
Leaves gossip like a chatty tour.
Whispers tickle, rustle, sway,
Making mischief, come what may.

Breezes carry tales so bright,
Tickling branches, oh what a sight!
A leaf drops, causing much ado,
'Watch your step!' a wise one blew.

Sunbeams dance like youthful jest,
Every flutter, nature's quest.
They giggle and tease the bough,
'We're on a roll, look at us now!'

Underneath the sky's embrace,
Leaves will wiggle, giggle, race.
In this shade, fun finds its way,
Come join us, in this leafy play!

Words Woven in Winds

In whispers soft, the breezes share,
Tricky tales with flair and dare.
A gust that shouts, 'You missed a beat!'
While flapping leaves dance to the beat.

Swaying branches tease with cheer,
'Don't you see? We're quite sincere!'
Each flutter sings a cheeky rhyme,
In this arboreal pantomime.

A leaf shifts, plays hide-and-seek,
Clean laundry flaps, we all peek.
'Oh, look at that one, trying to spin!'
Nature laughing at its whim.

Through sun and cloud, their antics rise,
A banquet of giggles, oh, what a prize!
In the wind's embrace, they weave their fable,
Join the merriment, if you're able!

Harmonies of Hues

In sea of greens, a vote today,
Who's the fairest in the fray?
Brown leaves chuckle at the gold,
'We've got stories yet untold!'

Scarlet blush reminds one of spice,
Singing, 'It's chilly — think twice!'
Orange dreams get up and schmooze,
Making merry in evening hues.

La la la, the palette beams,
As leaves conspire in shared dreams.
'You're too bright, tone down the scene!'
Purrs the whisper, sipping green.

Foliage dances, oh, what a song,
In this arboreal throng,
They sway and flutter with such flair,
A circus blooming everywhere!

Parables of the Past

Wise old oak sits, grinning wide,
Eavesdropping on the windy ride.
'Oh, the things I've seen with glee,
Let's spin a yarn, just you and me!'

Acorns chuckle, plotting schemes,
Turning tales of whimsical dreams.
'Once I strolled in yonder field,'
An oak storing stories, never sealed.

Maple whispers, 'Oh dear chap,
Let's spin a yarn, take a nap!'
As winds whirl fast with leaves in flight,
They recount antics, sheer delight.

From each branch to the roots below,
History's giggles, all aglow.
So join the laugh, don't stand and stare,
In this leafy lore, there's joy to share!

Chronicles of the Changing Shades

In autumn's breeze, they seem to joke,
A yellow leaf teased a green oak.
"You're just a sprout, but look at me!"
"I used to be fresh, oh can't you see?"

A squirrel chuckled, clutching a nut,
While chatting with a leaf, in a rut.
"You'll fall soon, then what will you be?"
"A carpet for folks, that's my spree!"

With each new hue, they start to dance,
In a swirling riot, a leaf's prance.
"Revamped outfits for every season!"
"Look at us now, with style and reason!"

As winter creeps, they shiver in glee,
Plotting fashion shows behind the tree.
"Think snow will stick? Or will we just sway?"
"No worries, we'll shine, come what may!"

Sounds of Silvan Harmony

Whispers in the woods, a leafy debate,
"Do you hear that? It's the pine's fate!"
The birches giggle, their trunks all aglow,
"Oh please, that's nothing, just old Bobo!"

Twirling in sync, a farce in the trees,
Maples sing high, "Sing us a tease!"
The oaks roll their bark, "Keep it down, chums!"
While spruces say, "Bark louder, here it comes!"

Chirps and chuckles, in rustling arrays,
It's a leafy ball, with shorts and berets!
"Oh what a party, turn up the breeze!"
And the willows sway like they've got the keys!

At dusk they plot, next week's big show,
"You bring the twigs, I'll bring the glow!"
In harmony hidden, mischief runs free,
Who knew the foliage had such esprit?

Signals from the Shade

Under the canopy, tricks unfold,
The leaves are gossiping, and it's pure gold.
"Did you see the beetle, with shiny attire?"
"Looks more like a wreck from the tire fire!"

The acorns chuckle, dropped in the fray,
"Bet the squirrels can't handle our ballet!"
As a winded leaf twirls, it shouts with flair,
"Catch me if you can, if you dare!"

A dance party brews, as dusk turns to night,
With shadows and winks, setting spirits alight.
"Lose a bit more, we'll pile up high!"
Chiming and chattering under the sky.

A breeze sighs softly, sharing the news,
"Let's crown the shadiest, pass me the dues!"
And under the starry, leafy embrace,
There's laughter and light, in this wild place!

Murmurs of the Wild

In the wild woods, where whispers reside,
Leaves gossip like friends, no place to hide.
"Did you hear the news? The wind changed its tune!"
"Sounded like the squirrels, howling at the moon!"

Grass blades laugh, in a ticklish spree,
While clovers exchange, secret jokes by the tree.
"Let's throw a shade, just for fun,
Watch out for sunbeams, they'd run!"

With fog rising up, and shadows at play,
Each branch wraps a tale, a raucous ballet.
"Did the mushrooms see? What a sight!"
"Nope, too busy jamming, all through the night!"

As leaves fall down, to the ground's warm embrace,
They giggle together, a wild, leafy race.
In the realm of the trees, where irony thrives,
Every rustle's a whisper, where laughter survives!

The Poetry of Foliage

In the breeze the leaves do dance,
Whispering secrets like a romance.
One says, 'Hey, what's your story?'
The other laughs, 'I'm an old glory!'

Shadows play games on the ground,
As squirrels giggle, all around.
A leaf would sigh, 'It's a wild ride!'
'Think I'll take an airborne slide!'

In a pile, they lovingly rest,
Each bright hue puts joy to the test.
Giggles erupt as they hear a call,
'Catch me if you can! Come, one and all!'

And trees above shake their heads,
'With such folly, you'll wake the dead!'
Yet leaves just chuckle, with twinkling prance,
'Let's keep the fun, it's leaf romance!'

Echoes of the Forest Floor

Beneath the trees, a giggle flows,
Leaves whisper low in theatrical prose.
A clumsy deer trips on a root,
Laughs echo as he regains his pursuit.

The mushrooms pop up, sporting a hat,
They turn and say, 'What of that?'
A cheeky breeze gives a playful shove,
'Keep it light, like a pushy dove!'

A chipmunk dances, his tail a plume,
While acorns declare, 'We're set to boom!'
Nature's orchestra plays without a care,
In this leafy world where giggles flare.

Woodpeckers knocking keep time with glee,
'Knock-knock jokes, who's there? It's me!'
Nature's humor, in every nook,
Leaves can chuckle, take a look!'

Harmonies of the Woodland

In the glen where sunlight peeks,
Leaves gossip softly, sharing tweaks.
One sings out, 'Look at my shine!'
'the sun kissed me, ain't I divine?'

A butterfly flutters and joins the fun,
'This party's great, I'm the spun!'
They tumble along in nature's art,
Like silly children, the leaves take part.

Gnarled branches nod, a wise old crew,
'With laughs in the air, we renew!'
A ripple of laughter runs through the throng,
'This forest jam is where we belong!'

So join the chorus, don your cheer,
In this woodland, there's nothing to fear.
With each rustle, memories pang,
Nature's music, in harmony, sang!'

Strokes of Nature's Brush

In colors that dance on a canvas bright,
Leaves paint the morning in pure delight.
A splash of gold, a stroke of green,
They laugh together in every scene.

A wind gust blows, what chaos it brings!
'Let's jump and spin, oh what wild flings!'
They swirl in whirlwinds, a colorful race,
Each leaf grinning, a cheeky face.

Crickets chirp in a tapping beat,
As nature's band resumes the heat.
Lo, the branches sway with flair,
Tickling the air, a comedic affair!

So gather your joy, let laughter flow,
In this leafy world, you'll steal the show.
With brushes of life, we paint and we jest,
In nature's art, we find our quest!'

Reflections in Rustling Leaves

Whispering secrets, they chirp and shout,
A gossip session without any doubt.
Pine needles rolling, a game on the ground,
Who knew that trees loved to clown all around?

Acorns are nutty, with jokes tough to crack,
While branches stretch out, they all break their back.
Maples are blushing, like they spilled some tea,
Tree trunks are snickering, so playful and free!

In breezes they twirl, the leaves dance in time,
Unruly performers in nature's grand mime.
From rustling murmurs to fluttery flips,
Each leaf has a punchline that rolls off their tips.

In the fall, they tumble, in a whirlwind of cheer,
Acting like they're all on a wacky career.
Their jokes, like confetti, will drift on the breeze,
Laughter in colors, oh what a tease!

The Sound of Sprouting

Listen closely, a giggle's in bloom,
Tiny new shoots, they joyfully zoom.
Sprouts peek from soil, all sprightly and bold,
With whispers of fun in the green underworld.

Worms having waltzes, beneath leafy bands,
Pulling the roots like they're holding hands.
The daisies are dainty, the tulips just grin,
As sunlight plays tag with a bright cheeky wind.

Squirrels salute as they shuffle on by,
Sticks waving wildly, in a cheerful tie.
With each little bud, a chuckle appears,
Nature's elite with their laughter through tears.

Each shoot and each leaf has a tale to present,
In this verdant circus, it's all heaven-sent.
From whispers to roars, let the laughter abound,
For the sprouts and the blooms make the funniest sound!

Monologues of Moss

Mossy philosophers sitting with grace,
Holding deep thoughts in their green, squishy space.
In shadows they linger, with wisdom in tow,
Making puns about fungi, as the breezes blow.

They've mastered the art of the slow, steady chat,
Musing on raindrops that fall from the hat.
"Did you hear the one about the leaf that took flight?
Got lost in the wind, and never came right!"

In corners they chuckle, a bashful brigade,
Fluffs of low humor, in the dimness they wade.
Their green velvet drama, a comedic delight,
In a cozy, green world that's silent at night.

"Why don't we travel?" one moss calls aloud,
"We're stuck here on stumps, it's just not allowed!"
With giggles of growth, just watch them unfold,
For wisdom in moss is a treasure untold.

A Symphony of Green Tones

A concerto of colors, each leaf plays a part,
With rustling melodies fresh from the heart.
The oak strums a bassline, deep and profound,
While willows serenade with their soft, swaying sound.

Bamboo's upbeat rhythm, like claps in the air,
Gives energy quickly, a lively affair.
While tulips soft whistle a sweet little tune,
Under the watch of a giggling moon.

As flowers harmonize, the breeze takes its cue,
Tickling the petals with notes tried and true.
Nature's orchestra gathers, all instruments keen,
With rustles and chuckles from the leafy green scene.

And when the sun sets, they all take a bow,
For it's nature's own show, and oh how they wow!
In a symphony swelling, their laughter is bold,
The music of leaves, a joy to behold!

www.ingramcontent.com/pod-product-compliance
Lightning Source LLC
Chambersburg PA
CBHW050317100526
44585CB00016BA/1564